SACRED READING

for Advent and Christmas
2017–2018

"For Advent 2016 and Lent 2017, we sent a copy of the Sacred Reading books to our parishioners' homes. Both editions have been well received by our community. They have helped us to grow in our prayer life through the sacred scripture. Sacred Reading helps parishioners to establish a prayer practice they can continue on their own, past the seasons of Advent and Lent."

Very Rev. Stephen D. Parkes, V.F.
Pastor of Annunciation Catholic Church
Altamonte Springs, Florida

SACRED READING

for Advent and Christmas
2017–2018

Apostleship of Prayer
The Pope's Worldwide Prayer Network

Douglas Leonard

AVE MARIA PRESS AVE Notre Dame, Indiana

Founded in 1865, Ave Maria Press is a ministry of the United States Province of Holy Cross.

www.avemariapress.com

Paperback: ISBN-13 978-1-59471-777-2

E-book: ISBN-13 978-1-59471-778-9

Cover design by Katherine J. Ross.

Text design by David Scholtes.

Printed and bound in the United States of America.

CONTENTS

INTRODUCTION

Advent is all about waiting for Jesus Christ. The gospel readings of Advent make us mindful of three ways we await Jesus—past, present, and future. First, we remember and accompany Mary, Joseph, and the newborn Jesus. Second, we prepare for the celebration of his birth this Christmas so that the day doesn't pass us by with just meaningless words and worthless presents. Third, we anticipate the second coming of Jesus Christ, who will come in power and glory for everyone to see and establish his kingdom of peace and justice upon the earth.

Christ is born, and we follow him in exile and in those joyful early years with the Holy Family. We are blessed, but we are challenged, too, to understand the ways of God and how we personally may understand and respond to them now.

One of the ways we can better understand and respond to the Lord during this holy season of Advent is by rediscovering, along with Christians all over the world, a powerful, ancient form of prayer known as *sacred reading*, also called "lectio divina." What better way to deepen one's friendship with Jesus Christ, the Word of God, than by prayerfully encountering him in the daily gospel? This book will set you on a personal prayer journey with Jesus.

Sacred Reading takes up this ancient practice of lectio divina in order to help you to engage the words of the daily gospel, guided by the Holy Spirit. As you read and pray this way, you may find—as many others have—that the Lord speaks to you in intimate and surprising ways. The reason for this is simple: as we open our hearts to Jesus, he opens his heart to us.

St. Paul prays beautifully for his readers:

> For this reason I bow my knees before the Father, from whom every family in heaven and on earth takes its name. I pray that, according to the riches of his glory, he may grant that you may be strengthened in your inner being with power through his Spirit, and that Christ may dwell in your hearts through faith, as you are being rooted and grounded in love. I pray that you may have the power to comprehend, with all the saints, what is the breadth and length and height and depth, and to know the love of Christ that surpasses knowledge, so that you may be filled with all the fullness of God. (Eph 3:14–19)

How to Use This Book

This book will set you on a personal prayer journey with Jesus from the first day of Advent through Epiphany Sunday. Each weekday reflection begins with the date, and some include a reference to the solemnity, feast, or sometimes a memorial on that day for which there is a special lectionary gospel reading. When these are indicated, the regular lectionary gospel reading for that day has been replaced with the gospel reading used to celebrate the solemnity or feast. Sunday reflections include both the date and its place in the liturgical calendar; any Sunday reading that includes a reference to a feast day rather than its place in the liturgical calendar uses the gospel reading for the feast day. For the sake of simplicity, other feast days are not cited when their gospel reading has not been used.

In prayerful reading of the daily gospels you join your prayers with those of believers all over the world. Following the readings for Advent and the Christmas season, each day you will be invited to reflect on the gospel text for the day, following six simple but profound steps:

1. *Know that God is present with you and ready to converse.*

At all times God is everywhere, including where you are at this very moment. The human mind is incapable of fully grasping the mystery of God, but we do know some things about God from scripture. God is the transcendent ground of all being, invisible, eternal, and infinite in power. God is love, with infinite love for you and me. God is one with and revealed through the Word, Jesus Christ, who became flesh. Through him all things were made, and by him and for him all things subsist. Jesus is the way, the truth, and the life. He says that those who know him also know his Father. Through the passion, death, and resurrection of Jesus, we are reconciled with God. If we believe in Jesus Christ, we become the sons and daughters of almighty God.

God gives us the Holy Spirit to lead us to truth and understanding. The Holy Spirit also gives us power to live obediently to the teachings of Jesus. The Holy Spirit draws us to prayer and works in us as we pray. No wonder we come into God's presence with gladness. All God's ways are good and beautiful. We can get to know God better by encountering God in the Word, Jesus himself.

The prompt prayer at the beginning of each day's reading is just that—a prompt, something to get you started. In fact, all the elements in the process of sacred reading are meant to prompt you to your own conversations with God. After reading the prompt, feel free to continue to pray in your own words: respond in your own way, pray in your own way, and hear God speaking to you personally. Your goal is to make sacred reading your own prayer time each day.

2. Read the Gospel.

The entire Bible is the Word of God, but the gospels (Matthew, Mark, Luke, and John) specifically tell the Good News about Jesus Christ. Throughout the Church year, the daily gospel readings during Mass will come from all four gospels. Sacred reading concentrates on praying with the daily gospels. These readings contain the story of Jesus' life, his teachings, his works, his Passion and Death on the Cross, his Resurrection on the third day, and his Ascension into heaven.

The gospels interpret Jesus' ministry for us. Much more, by the Holy Spirit, we can find in the gospels the very person of Jesus Christ. Prayerful reading of the daily gospel is an opportunity to draw close to the Lord—Father, Son, and Holy Spirit. As we pray with the gospels, we can be transformed by the grace of God—enlightened, strengthened, and moved. Seek to read the gospel with a complete openness to what God is saying to you. Many who pray with the gospel recommend rereading it several times.

3. Notice what you think and feel as you read the gospel.

Sacred reading can involve every faculty—mind, heart, emotions, soul, spirit, sensations, imagination, and much more—though usually not all at once. Different passages touch different keys in us. Sometimes we may laugh. Sometimes we may need to stop and worship before we continue. Sometimes we will be puzzled, amazed, stung, abashed, reminded of something lovely, or reminded of something we had wanted to forget.

Seek to feel all of your emotions as you read. Apply your intellect, too. You will confront problems of context and exegesis on a daily basis. That's okay. Sometimes you may experience very little. That's okay, too. God is at work anyway. Give yourself to the gospel and take from it what is there for you each day.

Most important, notice what in particular jumps out at you, whatever it may be. It may be a word, a phrase, a character, an image, a pattern, an emotion, a sensation—some arrow to your heart. Whatever it is, pay attention to it, because the Holy Spirit is using it to accomplish something in you.

Sometimes a particular gospel repeats during the liturgical year of the Church. To pray through the same gospel even on successive days presents no problem whatsoever to your sacred reading. St. Ignatius of Loyola, founder of the Jesuits and author of *The Spiritual Exercises*, actually recommends repeated meditation on passages of scripture. Read in the Spirit, gospel passages have unlimited potential to reveal to us the truths we are ready to receive. For the receptive soul, the Word of God has boundless power to illuminate and transform the prayerful believer.

4. *Pray as you are led for yourself and others.*

Praying is just talking with God. Believe God hears you. Believe God will answer you. Believe God knows what you need even before you ask. Jesus says so in the gospel. So, your conversation with God can go far beyond asking for things. You may thank, praise, worship, rejoice, mourn, explain, question, reveal your fears, seek understanding, or ask forgiveness. Your conversation with God has no limits. God is the ideal conversationalist. God wants to spend much time with you.

Being human, we can't help being self-absorbed, but praying is not just about our own needs. We are often moved by the gospel to pray for others. Often we will remember our loved ones in prayer. Sometimes we will be led to pray for someone who has hurt us. Sometimes we are moved to pray for a class of people in need, wherever they are in the world, such as for persecuted Christians, refugees, the mentally ill, the rich, teachers, the unborn, or the lonely.

We may also pray with the universal Church by praying for the pope's prayer intentions. Those intentions are entrusted to the Apostleship of Prayer and are available through its website and its annual and monthly leaflets. You may get your own copy of this year's papal prayer intentions by contacting the Apostleship of Prayer. The Apostleship is the pope's prayer group and has more than thirty-five million members worldwide. Jesus asked us to unite in prayer, promising that the Father would grant us whatever we ask for in his name.

5. *Listen to Jesus.*

Jesus the Good Shepherd speaks to his own sheep, who hear his voice (see Jn 10:27). The passages in step five are words I felt impressed upon my heart as I prayed with these readings. I included them in order to help you listen for whatever it is the Lord might be saying to you.

This listening is a most wonderful time in your sacred reading prayer experience. Jesus speaks to all in the gospels, but in your sacred reading prayer experience he can now speak exclusively to you. If you can, write down what he says to you and reread his words during the day. Put all of Jesus' words to you in a folder or keep a spiritual notebook. Believers through the ages have recorded the words of Jesus to them, holy mystics and ordinary believers alike.

It takes faith to hear the voice of Jesus. This faith will grow as you practice listening. Ideally, we will learn to hear what Jesus is saying to us all day long—as we face difficult situations perhaps. Listening to the voice of Jesus is practicing the presence of God. As St. Paul said, "In him we live and move and have our being" (Acts 17:28).

St. Ignatius of Loyola called this conversation with Jesus *colloquy*. That word simply means that two or more people are talking. St. Ignatius even urges us to include the saints in our prayer conversations. We believe in the Communion of Saints. If you have a patron saint, don't be afraid to talk to him or her. In her autobiography, St. Thérèse of Lisieux, who was a member of the Apostleship of Prayer, describes how she spoke often with Mary and Joseph, as well as with Jesus.

6. *Ask God to show you how to live today.*

Pope Benedict XVI commented that sacred reading is not complete without a call to action; something in our praying leads us to do something in our day. Perhaps we find an opportunity to serve, to love, to give, to lead, or to do something good for someone else. Perhaps we find occasion to repent, to forgive, to ask forgiveness, to make amends. Open your heart to anything God might want you to do. Try to keep the conversation with God going all day long.

"Ask God to show you how to live today" is the last step of the sacred reading prayer time, but that doesn't mean you need to end it there. Keep it going. You may drift off in the presence of God, lose attention, or even fall asleep, but you can come back. God is always present, seeking to love you and to be loved. God is always seeking to lead us to green pastures. God is our strength, our rock, our ever-present help in time of trouble. God is full of mercy, ready to forgive us again and again. God sees us through very difficult times. God heals us. God gives his life to us constantly. God is our Maker, Father, Mother, Lover, Servant, Savior, and Friend. We know that from the gospel. He is an inexhaustible spring of blessing and holiness in our innermost selves. The sanctification of our souls is God's work, not our own.

As you read, ask the Holy Spirit to lead you in this process. With genuine faith, open yourself to respond to the Word and the Spirit, and your relationship with Jesus will continue to deepen and to grow just as the infant Jesus grew within the womb of the Blessed Mother. This in turn will lead you to share the love of Christ with all those you encounter—just as the Blessed Mother draws all those who encounter her directly to her Son.

Other Resources to Help You

These Sacred Reading resources, including both the seasonal books and the annual prayer book, are enriched by the spirituality of the Apostleship of Prayer. Since 1844, our mission has been to encourage Catholics to pray each day for the good of the world, the Church, and the prayer intentions of the Holy Father. In particular, we encourage Christians to respond to the loving gift of Jesus Christ by making a daily offering of themselves. As we give him our hearts, we ask that he may make them like his own heart, full of love, mercy, and peace.

These booklets may be used in small groups or as a handy individual resource for those who want a special way to draw close to Christ during Advent. If you enjoy these reflections and would like to continue this prayerful reading throughout the year, pick up a copy of the *Sacred Reading* annual prayer guide at the website of the Apostleship of Prayer or avemariapress.com. These annual books offer a personal prayer experience that can be adapted to meet your particular needs. For example, some choose to continue to reflect in writing, either in the book or in a separate journal or notebook, to create a record of their spiritual journey for the entire year. Others supplement their daily reading from the book with the daily videos and other online resources available through the Apostleship of Prayer website.

If you are new to the practice of daily prayer or would like more information about a different kind of daily prayer offering, we have also included at the end of this booklet and excerpt from another Apostleship of Prayer resource, *Three Moments of the Day* by Christopher S. Collins, S.J. This book is a wonderful introduction to another form of Ignatian prayer that is central to spirituality of the Apostleship of Prayer, the morning offering.

For more information about the Apostleship of Prayer and about the other resources we have developed to help men and women cultivate habits of daily prayer, visit our website at apostleshipofprayer.org.

I pray that this experience may help you walk closely with God every day.

Douglas Leonard, PhD
Apostleship of Prayer

FIRST WEEK OF ADVENT

The heart of Mary, more than any other, is a humble heart, capable of accepting God's gifts. In order to become man, God chose precisely her, a simple young woman of Nazareth, who did not dwell in the palaces of power and wealth, who did not do extraordinary things. Let us ask ourselves—it will do us good—if we are prepared to accept God's gifts, or prefer instead to shut ourselves up within our forms of material security, intellectual security, the security of our plans.

Pope Francis
October 9, 2016

Sunday, December 3, 2017
First Sunday of Advent

Know that God is present
and ready to converse.

The Church has waited many centuries for the Lord to return in power and glory. Anticipating that, Jesus exhorts us not to grow discouraged or slacken in our duties. We are to expect his return at all times, staying awake, and serving him in the people of our lives.

"Lord God of Abraham, Father of Jesus, you are Love, and you are with me now. Teach me by your Word."

Read the gospel: Mark 13:33–37.

Jesus said, "Beware, keep alert; for you do not know when the time will come. It is like a man going on a journey, when he leaves home and puts his slaves in charge, each with his work, and commands the door-keeper to be on the watch. Therefore, keep awake—for you do not know when the master of the house will come, in the evening, or at midnight, or at cockcrow, or at dawn, or else he may find you asleep when he comes suddenly. And what I say to you I say to all: Keep awake."

Notice what you think and feel
as you read the gospel.

Jesus understands how hard it is to wait for him, yet he demands it. And even so, he will return unexpect-edly—unexpectedly, at least, for those who are not watching and waiting.

Pray as you are led for yourself and others.

"Lord, throughout history, until John the Baptist, Jews waited for your coming. You came as a baby. Thank you. Help me to stay awake until you come again. Let those you have given me be ready, too . . ." (Continue in your own words.)

Listen to Jesus.

I am the Alpha and the Omega, my beloved child. I am your beginning and your end. Rest in me. What else is Jesus saying to you?

Ask God to show you how to live today.

"Open my eyes, Lord; awaken me to your presence. Amen."

Monday, December 4, 2017

Know that God is present and ready to converse.

"Lord, in your greatness you condescend to give me life, and life more abundantly, through your Son, Jesus, the Word of God."

Read the gospel: Matthew 8:5–11.

When Jesus entered Capernaum, a centurion came to him, appealing to him and saying, "Lord, my servant is lying at home paralyzed, in terrible distress." And he said to him, "I will come and cure him." The centurion answered, "Lord, I am not worthy to have you come under my roof; but only speak the word, and my servant will be healed. For I also am a man under authority, with soldiers under me; and I say to one, 'Go,' and he goes, and to another, 'Come,' and he comes, and to my slave, 'Do this,' and the slave does it." When Jesus heard him, he was amazed and said to those who followed him, "Truly I tell you, in no one in Israel have I found such faith. I tell you, many will come from east and west and will eat with Abraham and Isaac and Jacob in the kingdom of heaven."

Notice what you think and feel as you read the gospel.

Jesus responds to the centurion's humility, but, even more, he is "amazed" by his faith. Faith is the key to the kingdom of heaven.

Pray as you are led for yourself and others.

"Lord, humility and faith are virtues, and all virtues flow from God as gifts to us. I pray for the virtues of faith, hope, and love not just for myself but also for . . ." (Continue in your own words.)

Listen to Jesus.

You know my mind; you speak my heart, beloved disciple. I long for the salvation of all those you love. What else is Jesus saying to you?

Ask God to show you how to live today.

"Give me the faith to be obedient to you, Lord, that my actions may bring others your love and healing. I glorify you, Jesus. Amen."

Tuesday, December 5, 2017

Know that God is present and ready to converse.

"You know me, Father; how may I know you? I will listen to your Word."

Read the gospel: Luke 10:21–24.

At that same hour Jesus rejoiced in the Holy Spirit and said, "I thank you, Father, Lord of heaven and earth, because you have hidden these things from the wise and the intelligent and have revealed them to infants; yes, Father, for such was your gracious will. All things have been handed over to me by my Father; and no one knows who the Son is except the Father, or who the Father is except the Son and anyone to whom the Son chooses to reveal him."

Then turning to the disciples, Jesus said to them privately, "Blessed are the eyes that see what you see! For I tell you that many prophets and kings desired to see what you see, but did not see it, and to hear what you hear, but did not hear it."

Notice what you think and feel as you read the gospel.

Jesus thanks his Father that he has hidden divine truths from intelligent people and revealed them to children. Only the Son can reveal God to us. And the Son is willing to bless us. Then he speaks to his disciples privately about their privilege.

Pray as you are led for yourself and others.

"I am sorry for thinking I understand things, Lord. I know nothing apart from what you teach me. Help my heart receive your Spirit. Help others . . ." (Continue in your own words.)

Listen to Jesus.

The world waited for me but did not know me when I came. I am among you now, and the world still does not know me. Join the saints in heaven in praying for those who do not know me. What else is Jesus saying to you?

Ask God to show you how to live today.

"You are right that I don't know how to show you to those who do not know you. Give me opportunity, words, action, and courage to show love to one of those today. Amen."

Wednesday, December 6, 2017

Know that God is present and ready to converse.

"Jesus, Bread of Life, let your Word be the bread of my life today."

Read the gospel: Matthew 15:29–37.

After Jesus had left that place, he passed along the Sea of Galilee, and he went up the mountain, where he sat down. Great crowds came to him, bringing with them the lame, the maimed, the blind, the mute, and many others. They put them at his feet, and he cured them, so that the crowd was amazed when they saw the mute speaking, the maimed whole, the lame walking, and the blind seeing. And they praised the God of Israel.

Then Jesus called his disciples to him and said, "I have compassion for the crowd, because they have been with me now for three days and have nothing to eat; and I do not want to send them away hungry, for they might faint on the way." The disciples said to him, "Where are we to get enough bread in the desert to feed so great a crowd?" Jesus asked them, "How many loaves have you?" They said, "Seven, and a few small fish." Then ordering the crowd to sit down on the ground, he took the seven loaves and the fish; and after giving thanks he broke them and gave them to the disciples, and the disciples gave them to the crowds. And all of them ate and were filled; and they took up the broken pieces left over, seven baskets full.

Notice what you think and feel as you read the gospel.

In compassion for the crowd in the deserted place, Jesus feeds them all, multiplying the loaves and fish. Strangely, no one seems surprised that it is happening. Did they not realize?

Pray as you are led for yourself and others.

"Lord, how much do I not realize how you work among us. Forgive me for not seeing and trusting your compassion for me and for all you have given me . . ." (Continue in your own words.)

Listen to Jesus.

I am feeding you, beloved. Come to me every day, and I will give you secret bread I have reserved for only you. What else is Jesus saying to you?

Ask God to show you how to live today.

"Let my heart, mind, words, and actions be full of you today, gracious Lord, loving Jesus. Amen."

Thursday, December 7, 2017

Know that God is present and ready to converse.

"Lord, show me how to please you and remain in you."

Read the gospel: Matthew 7:21, 24–27.

Jesus said, "Not everyone who says to me, 'Lord, Lord,' will enter the kingdom of heaven, but only one who does the will of my Father in heaven. . . .

"Everyone then who hears these words of mine and acts on them will be like a wise man who built his house on rock. The rain fell, the floods came, and the winds blew and beat on that house, but it did not fall, because it had been founded on rock. And everyone who hears these words of mine and does not act on them will be like a foolish man who built his house on sand. The rain fell, and the floods came, and the winds blew and beat against that house, and it fell—and great was its fall!"

Notice what you think and feel as you read the gospel.

Jesus tells us how to get to heaven: do the will of his Father—hear the word of God and act upon it. This takes daily effort, faith, and commitment. This is how we build our house on the Rock of Jesus.

Pray as you are led for yourself and others.

"Jesus, you are very clear in this teaching. Forgive me for the times I sought my own will, would not listen to you, would not act upon your words. I offer myself to you now for conversion . . ." (Continue in your own words.)

Listen to Jesus.

My beloved, you are mine and I care for you. I set you on solid ground and build you up. What else is Jesus saying to you?

Ask God to show you how to live today.

"Show me the will of the Father, Jesus, and give me the strength to carry it out. Amen."

Friday, December 8, 2017
Immaculate Conception of the Blessed Virgin Mary

Know that God is present and ready to converse.

"Here I am, mighty Spirit of Holiness. Be it done to me according to your Word."

Read the gospel: Luke 1:26–38.

In the sixth month the angel Gabriel was sent by God to a town in Galilee called Nazareth, to a virgin engaged to a man whose name was Joseph, of the house of David. The virgin's name was Mary. And he came to her and said, "Greetings, favored one! The Lord is with you." But she was much perplexed by his words and pondered what sort of greeting this might be. The angel said to her, "Do not be afraid, Mary, for you have found favor with God. And now, you will conceive in your womb and bear a son, and you will name him Jesus. He will be great, and will be called the Son of the Most High, and the Lord God will give to him the throne of his ancestor David. He will reign over the house of Jacob forever, and of his kingdom there will be no end." Mary said to the angel, "How can this be, since I am a virgin?" The angel said to her, "The Holy Spirit will come upon you, and the power of the Most High will overshadow you; therefore the child to be born will be holy; he will be called Son of God. And now, your relative Elizabeth in her old age has also conceived a son; and this is the sixth month for her who was said to be barren. For nothing will be impossible with God." Then Mary said, "Here am I, the servant of the Lord; let it be with me according to your word." Then the angel departed from her.

Notice what you think and feel as you read the gospel.

In a single moment, Mary's plan for her life is demolished by an angel's perplexing message. How can this be? But she soon understands it doesn't matter what she understands—she makes herself absolutely available to God for whatever God wills, even if it is "impossible."

Pray as you are led for yourself and others.

"Thy will be done, Lord, in earth as in heaven, and in me as in Mary. I surrender, and with your grace I will be able to give myself more fully each day. I am also giving to you today those you have given me, that you may do your will in them . . ." (Continue in your own words.)

Listen to Jesus.

God is good, beloved servant, God knows what you need before you ask, and God has granted your prayers today. What else is Jesus saying to you?

Ask God to show you how to live today.

"Help me be aware of moments when I need to stop wondering and just bow to your will with grateful acceptance. Give me grace to trust you in my circumstances. Thank you. Amen."

Saturday, December 9, 2017

Know that God is present and ready to converse.

"Lord, may your Word move my heart to love you and my will to action—action that serves others as you would have me serve."

Read the gospel: Matthew 9:35–10:1, 5a, 6–8.

Then Jesus went about all the cities and villages, teaching in their synagogues, and proclaiming the good news of the kingdom, and curing every disease and every sickness. When he saw the crowds, he had compassion for them, because they were harassed and helpless, like sheep without a shepherd. Then he said to his disciples, "The harvest is plentiful, but the laborers are few; therefore ask the Lord of the harvest to send out laborers into his harvest."

Then Jesus summoned his twelve disciples and gave them authority over unclean spirits, to cast them out, and to cure every disease and every sickness. . . .

These twelve Jesus sent out with the following instructions: ". . . Go rather to the lost sheep of the house of Israel. As you go, proclaim the good news, 'The kingdom of heaven has come near.' Cure the sick, raise the dead, cleanse the lepers, cast out demons. You received without payment; give without payment."

Notice what you think and feel as you read the gospel.

The people are "harassed and helpless," Jesus says, and he wishes to provide them shepherds. He gives the twelve power and sends them out to preach and do wonders not for personal gain, but only to show the love of God and the truth of the kingdom.

Pray as you are led for yourself and others.

"So many now are harassed and helpless, in poverty, sickness, war, persecution, violence, abuse, addiction, prison. Lord, send laborers to bring them relief and knowledge of you . . ." (Continue in your own words.)

Listen to Jesus.

You see how nothing has changed, my child? This world needs redemption that comes only through God. When will people turn to me? What else is Jesus saying to you?

Ask God to show you how to live today.

"Lord, how can I help? Send me. Amen."

SECOND WEEK OF ADVENT

When God comes to encounter us, he moves us inwardly; he sets in motion what we are until our whole life is transformed into praise and blessing. When God visits us, he leaves us restless, with the healthy restlessness of those who feel they have been called to proclaim that he lives and is in the midst of his people.

Pope Francis
December 12, 2016

Sunday, December 10, 2017
Second Sunday of Advent

Know that God is present
and ready to converse.

John the Baptist is a fascinating figure in the unfolding of God's plan to visit his people in Person. For all his charisma, he has a limited role that requires great humility and incredible courage. His preaching of repentance led to his martyrdom.

"Lord, by your Spirit and your Word, you raise up holy men and women to serve you. I am ready to hear you now because I know you can do all things, even in me."

Read the gospel: Mark 1:1–8.

The beginning of the good news of Jesus Christ, the Son of God.

As it is written in the prophet Isaiah,

"See, I am sending my messenger ahead of you,
   who will prepare your way;
the voice of one crying out in the wilderness:
   'Prepare the way of the Lord,
   make his paths straight.'"

John the baptizer appeared in the wilderness, proclaiming a baptism of repentance for the forgiveness of sins. And people from the whole Judean countryside and all the people of Jerusalem were going out to him, and were baptized by him in the river Jordan, confessing their sins. Now John was clothed with camel's hair, with a leather belt around his waist, and he ate locusts and wild honey. He proclaimed, "The one who is more powerful than I is coming after me; I am not worthy to stoop down and untie the thong of his sandals. I have baptized you with water; but he will baptize you with the Holy Spirit."

Notice what you think and feel as you read the gospel.

This is the beginning of the Good News of the Kingdom of God. John must have appeared as a wild man, yet people flocked to him in the wilderness, repented, and were baptized. John told them about the greater, more powerful One who was to follow.

Pray as you are led for yourself and others.

"Lord, let repentance be the first step for me, too, so I will be ready for your baptism with the Holy Spirit. I pray that all sinners see their need to repent and then do so. I think of . . ." (Continue in your own words.)

Listen to Jesus.

I long to open the eyes of the blind, to soften the hearts of the hard-hearted. I invite whoever will hear to come to me and be baptized into the kingdom. Pray with me for sinners. What else is Jesus saying to you?

Ask God to show you how to live today.

"Remind me and I will pray for sinners many times today, saying 'Have mercy upon us, Lord.' Remind me, Jesus. Thank you for asking me to serve. Amen."

Monday, December 11, 2017

Know that God is present and ready to converse.

"Jesus Christ, let me spare no effort to come to you every day. I need your healing touch."

Read the gospel: Luke 5:17–26.

One day, while Jesus was teaching, Pharisees and teachers of the law were sitting nearby (they had come from every village of Galilee and Judea and from Jerusalem); and the power of the Lord was with him to heal. Just then some men came, carrying a paralyzed man on a bed. They were trying to bring him in and lay him before Jesus; but finding no way to bring him in because of the crowd, they went up on the roof and let him down with his bed through the tiles into the middle of the crowd in front of Jesus. When he saw their faith, he said, "Friend, your sins are forgiven you." Then the scribes and the Pharisees began to question, "Who is this who is speaking blasphemies? Who can forgive sins but God alone?" When Jesus perceived their questionings, he answered them, "Why do you raise such questions in your hearts? Which is easier, to say, 'Your sins are forgiven you,' or to say, 'Stand up and walk'? But so that you may know that the Son of Man has authority on earth to forgive sins"—he said to the one who was paralyzed— "I say to you, stand up and take your bed and go to your home." Immediately he stood up before them, took what he had been lying on, and went to his home, glorifying God. Amazement seized all of them, and they glorified God and were filled with awe, saying, "We have seen strange things today."

Notice what you think and feel as you read the gospel.

Because Jesus is Emmanuel, God with us, he can both heal infirmities of the body and forgive sins of the soul. The scribes and Pharisees do not understand that, and Jesus makes his identity clear to them, even though they may not receive it. Yet all present are filled with awe and glorify God.

Pray as you are led for yourself and others.

"Lord, let me be lowered down before you, so you can heal me and forgive my sins. I need you. Others need you, too, so I pray . . ." (Continue in your own words.)

Listen to Jesus.

Servant, I am always here to heal you and wash you clean. I love you. Our love is the most important thing. I am happy when you show your love to me. What else is Jesus saying to you?

Ask God to show you how to live today.

"I am awed that you love me—and grateful, for I am but sinful flesh and blood. Be with me, loving Savior, and I will do your will today. Amen."

Tuesday, December 12, 2017
Our Lady of Guadalupe

Know that God is present and ready to converse.

"Lord God of Hosts, Master of the Universe, you stoop to live among the humble of the earth. Let me be one of them."

Read the gospel: Luke 1:26–38.

In the sixth month the angel Gabriel was sent by God to a town in Galilee called Nazareth, to a virgin engaged to a man whose name was Joseph, of the house of David. The virgin's name was Mary. And he came to her and said, "Greetings, favored one! The Lord is with you." But she was much perplexed by his words and pondered what sort of greeting this might be. The angel said to her, "Do not be afraid, Mary, for you have found favor with God. And now, you will conceive in your womb and bear a son, and you will name him Jesus. He will be great, and will be called the Son of the Most High, and the Lord God will give to him the throne of his ancestor David. He will reign over the house of Jacob forever, and of his kingdom there will be no end." Mary said to the angel, "How can this be, since I am a virgin?" The angel said to her, "The Holy Spirit will come upon you, and the power of the Most High will overshadow you; therefore the child to be born will be holy; he will be called Son of God. And now, your relative Elizabeth in her old age has also conceived a son; and this is the sixth month for her who was said to be barren. For nothing will be impossible with God." Then Mary said, "Here am I, the servant of the Lord; let it be with me according to your word." Then the angel departed from her.

Notice what you think and feel as you read the gospel.

The angel tells Mary she is favored by God, but what a world of woe lies in store for her! Yet through her comes Emmanuel, the Messiah, the Savior of the World, the King of Glory. Thus she is the Mother of God.

Pray as you are led for yourself and others.

"Lord, like Mary, I am sometimes perplexed by events in my life, all of which come from your hand. Help me to accept them, and let it be done unto me according to your will . . ." (Continue in your own words.)

Listen to Jesus.

Your role, my dear follower, is to make my will your own. You can accomplish this through prayer. I will bless you beyond what you can imagine. What else is Jesus saying to you?

Ask God to show you how to live today.

"Help me seek your will for me, Lord, and let my suffering be used to bring your kingdom into the world. Amen."

Wednesday, December 13, 2017

Know that God is present
and ready to converse.

"I come to you, Lord. Give me both rest and the power
to take your yoke upon myself."

Read the gospel: Matthew 11:28–30.

Jesus said, "Come to me, all you that are weary and are
carrying heavy burdens, and I will give you rest. Take
my yoke upon you, and learn from me; for I am gentle
and humble in heart, and you will find rest for your
souls. For my yoke is easy, and my burden is light."

Notice what you think and feel
as you read the gospel.

Jesus says he is gentle and humble of heart. Why? So
the weary and overburdened will not be afraid to come
to him for rest.

Pray as you are led for yourself and others.

"Gentle Jesus, I know you value humility. Strike down
all my pride and give me humility like yours. I cer-
tainly cannot manufacture it in myself. Then let me
take on the burdens of others . . ." (Continue in your
own words.)

Listen to Jesus.

*My heart is my love for you and for all humanity. I am
willing to give you my heart, friend, so that you may give it
to others. This is the only hope for the world.* What else is
Jesus saying to you?

Ask God to show you how to live today.

"Jesus, I am willing to receive your heart, and with your grace I will give it to others. Glory to you, O Lord. Amen."

Thursday, December 14, 2017

**Know that God is present
and ready to converse.**

"Lord, let me receive and accept your Word."

Read the gospel: Matthew 11:11–15.

Jesus said, "Truly I tell you, among those born of women no one has arisen greater than John the Baptist; yet the least in the kingdom of heaven is greater than he. From the days of John the Baptist until now the kingdom of heaven has suffered violence, and the violent take it by force. For all the prophets and the law prophesied until John came; and if you are willing to accept it, he is Elijah who is to come. Let anyone with ears listen!"

**Notice what you think and feel
as you read the gospel.**

I do not understand how the kingdom of heaven has suffered violence, and the violent take it by force. Yet Jesus implies that things have changed now, for he has opened the kingdom to all who heed the words of repentance and grace.

Pray as you are led for yourself and others.

"Lord, I aspire to be greater than John only in humility. Mold me to your will . . ." (Continue in your own words.)

Listen to Jesus.

Dear one, can you imagine my task of teaching men and women the power and glory of God? They accused me of speaking in riddles. Let me speak to you plainly now. I love you. I hear your prayers. Follow me. What else is Jesus saying to you?

Ask God to show you how to live today.

"Lord, I need your Holy Spirit even to receive your message of love. Help me apply your love in all I do. Amen."

Friday, December 15, 2017

**Know that God is present
and ready to converse.**

"Open my mind to your Word, Lord, for without your grace I will not understand it."

Read the gospel: Matthew 11:16–19.

Jesus said, "But to what will I compare this generation? It is like children sitting in the market-places and calling to one another,

> 'We played the flute for you, and you did not
> dance;
> we wailed, and you did not mourn.'

For John came neither eating nor drinking, and they say, 'He has a demon'; the Son of Man came eating and drinking, and they say, 'Look, a glutton and a drunkard, a friend of tax-collectors and sinners!' Yet wisdom is vindicated by her deeds."

Notice what you think and feel as you read the gospel.

Jesus complains that people won't receive God's message no matter how it's presented. They constantly find fault with the messenger. But, he concludes, after all is said and done, one's wisdom is proven by one's actions and deeds.

Pray as you are led for yourself and others.

"Move me to right action, Lord. Be a lamp to my feet. Strengthen my hands and heart for the labors of love you give me. Let me help . . ." (Continue in your own words.)

Listen to Jesus.

Blessed and wise is the one who does the will of God. Seek, beloved, to know and to do the will of God in your own life. What else is Jesus saying to you?

Ask God to show you how to live today.

"Then increase my desire for you, Jesus, and to do the Father's will. Help me act in your love. Amen."

Saturday, December 16, 2017

**Know that God is present
and ready to converse.**

"Jesus, beloved Son, let me listen to you and be filled with awe."

Read the gospel: Matthew 17:9a, 10–13.

As they were coming down the mountain, Jesus ordered them, "Tell no one about the vision until after the Son of Man has been raised from the dead." . . . And the disciples asked him, "Why, then, do the scribes say that Elijah must come first?" He replied, "Elijah is indeed coming and will restore all things; but I tell you that Elijah has already come, and they did not recognize him, but they did to him whatever they pleased. So also the Son of Man is about to suffer at their hands." Then the disciples understood that he was speaking to them about John the Baptist.

Notice what you think and feel as you read the gospel.

The disciples understand he is speaking about John, but they seem deaf to his mention about being raised from the dead, and deaf again at his mention of his own suffering. They would not fully understand until after it had happened, after they had seen it for themselves, and after the Holy Spirit fully informed them.

Pray as you are led for yourself and others.

"Jesus, I don't want to be deaf or in denial of truth. Open my understanding to what you deem I need to know, for I want to please you, not myself. I offer myself today for the good of those you have given me . . ." (Continue in your own words.)

Listen to Jesus.

I am ready to give every person the knowledge he or she needs, but the person must seek it with an open heart and mind. Some refuse to open to me. Pray for them, beloved. Thank you. What else is Jesus saying to you?

Ask God to show you how to live today.

"So I will spend many moments of my day praying for those who refuse to open to your truth and grace. Remind me to do so often, Lord. Praise God Almighty! Amen."

THIRD WEEK OF ADVENT

Hope is a gift of God. We must ask for it. It is placed deep within each human heart in order to shed light on this life, so often troubled and clouded by so many situations that bring sadness and pain. We need to nourish the roots of our hope so that they can bear fruit; primarily, the certainty of God's closeness and compassion, despite whatever evil we have done. There is no corner of our heart that cannot be touched by God's love. Whenever someone makes a mistake, the Father's mercy is all the more present, awakening repentance, forgiveness, reconciliation, and peace.

Pope Francis
November 6, 2016

Sunday, December 17, 2017
Third Sunday of Advent

Know that God is present
and ready to converse.

"Light of the world, light of my life, let me see you in your Word."

As the candles in the Advent wreath continue to burn during this time of hopeful anticipation, our longing for the Lord grows. We love the infant Jesus. We love the triumphant Messiah who is to come. But, best of all, for now and for eternity, we love the coming and abiding of Jesus Christ in our hearts. The kingdom of heaven is already within us.

"I welcome you into my day, Lord, though you are always with me. I am here with you."

Read the gospel: John 1:6–8, 19–28.

There was a man sent from God, whose name was John. He came as a witness to testify to the light, so that all might believe through him. He himself was not the light, but he came to testify to the light. . . .

This is the testimony given by John when the Jews sent priests and Levites from Jerusalem to ask him, "Who are you?" He confessed and did not deny it, but confessed, "I am not the Messiah." And they asked him, "What then? Are you Elijah?" He said, "I am not." "Are you the prophet?" He answered, "No." Then they said to him, "Who are you? Let us have an answer for those who sent us. What do you say about yourself?" He said,

"I am the voice of one crying out in the wilderness,
'Make straight the way of the Lord,'"

as the prophet Isaiah said.

Now they had been sent from the Pharisees. They
asked him, "Why then are you baptizing if you are
neither the Messiah, nor Elijah, nor the prophet?" John
answered them, "I baptize with water. Among you
stands one whom you do not know, the one who is
coming after me; I am not worthy to untie the thong
of his sandal." This took place in Bethany across the
Jordan where John was baptizing.

Notice what you think and feel as you read the gospel.

John has a positive message, for he proclaims the immi-
nent coming of the Lord. Those who hear him press
him for more, so he has to declare plainly that he is not
the Messiah, Elijah, or the prophet. He declares also
that he is not worthy to untie the thong of the sandal
of the one who is to come after him.

Pray as you are led for yourself and others.

"How human we are, Lord, as we dispute about your
words. Let me avoid dispute and with simple heart
and mind receive you. I pray others do as well . . ."
(Continue in your own words.)

Listen to Jesus.

*You see why I have said that intelligent people cannot under-
stand, while children can. Study to be a child, for you are my
child. Love and trust your Lord and God. All shall be well
with you and yours.* What else is Jesus saying to you?

Ask God to show you how to live today.

"By your grace, let me learn and practice simplicity, love, and trust today. Let it bring honor to you, Lord. Amen."

Monday, December 18, 2017

Know that God is present and ready to converse.

"Father in heaven, you sent your son out of love for us. You made yourself present in history and in the flesh. Thank you."

Read the gospel: Matthew 1:18–25.

Now the birth of Jesus the Messiah took place in this way. When his mother Mary had been engaged to Joseph, but before they lived together, she was found to be with child from the Holy Spirit. Her husband Joseph, being a righteous man and unwilling to expose her to public disgrace, planned to dismiss her quietly. But just when he had resolved to do this, an angel of the Lord appeared to him in a dream and said, "Joseph, son of David, do not be afraid to take Mary as your wife, for the child conceived in her is from the Holy Spirit. She will bear a son, and you are to name him Jesus, for he will save his people from their sins." All this took place to fulfill what had been spoken by the Lord through the prophet:

> "Look, the virgin shall conceive and bear a son,
>   and they shall name him 'Emmanuel,'

which means, 'God is with us.'"

When Joseph awoke from sleep, he did as the angel of the Lord commanded him; he took her as his wife, but had no marital relations with her until she had borne a son; and he named him Jesus.

Notice what you think and feel as you read the gospel.

More than half of the words of this gospel passage concern Joseph's dream. He went to sleep facing a personal crisis and a social crisis, too, with Mary's pregnancy. He awakens to follow not his own plans but what the angel commanded him. He married Mary, and they named the child Jesus.

Pray as you are led for yourself and others.

"Human predicaments sometimes seem impossible, but you can untangle the knots, Lord. I place before you my greatest knot today. Command me what to do, and give me grace to do it . . ." (Continue in your own words.)

Listen to Jesus.

You are right to seek me when you are in trouble of any kind. I love you, and I am willing and able to save you, and also those you pray for. Cast your cares upon me! What else is Jesus saying to you?

Ask God to show you how to live today.

"Let me return in prayer often today, Lord, as I turn my cares over to you. Thank you for your daily love and guidance. Amen."

Tuesday, December 19, 2017

Know that God is present and ready to converse.

"How marvelous are your ways and works, Lord. Open my eyes to adore you."

Read the gospel: Luke 1:5–25.

In the days of King Herod of Judea, there was a priest named Zechariah, who belonged to the priestly order of Abijah. His wife was a descendant of Aaron, and her name was Elizabeth. Both of them were righteous before God, living blamelessly according to all the commandments and regulations of the Lord. But they had no children, because Elizabeth was barren, and both were getting on in years.

Once when he was serving as priest before God and his section was on duty, he was chosen by lot, according to the custom of the priesthood, to enter the sanctuary of the Lord and offer incense. Now at the time of the incense-offering, the whole assembly of the people was praying outside. Then there appeared to him an angel of the Lord, standing at the right side of the altar of incense. When Zechariah saw him, he was terrified; and fear overwhelmed him. But the angel said to him, "Do not be afraid, Zechariah, for your prayer has been heard. Your wife Elizabeth will bear you a son, and you will name him John. You will have joy and gladness, and many will rejoice at his birth, for he will be great in the sight of the Lord. He must never drink wine or strong drink; even before his birth he will be filled with the Holy Spirit. He will turn many of the people of Israel to the Lord their God. With the spirit and power of Elijah he will go before him, to turn the hearts of parents to their children, and the disobedient to the wisdom of the righteous, to make ready a people prepared for the Lord." Zechariah said to the angel, "How will I know that this is so? For I am an old man, and my wife is getting on in years." The angel replied, "I am Gabriel. I stand in the presence of God, and I have been sent to speak to you and to bring you this good news. But now, because you did not believe my words, which will be fulfilled in their time, you will become mute, unable to speak, until the day these things occur."

Meanwhile, the people were waiting for Zechariah, and wondered at his delay in the sanctuary. When he did come out, he could not speak to them, and they realized that he had seen a vision in the sanctuary. He kept motioning to them and remained unable to speak. When his time of service was ended, he went to his home.

After those days his wife Elizabeth conceived, and for five months she remained in seclusion. She said, "This is what the Lord has done for me when he looked favorably on me and took away the disgrace I have endured among my people."

Notice what you think and feel as you read the gospel.

Zechariah hears the prophecy from the angel and is struck dumb for not believing. Despite his opinion that his aged wife cannot conceive, she does—just as the angel had said—and Elizabeth is joyful.

Pray as you are led for yourself and others.

"Lord, forgive me for being slow to believe your promises. They are so wonderful. I pray that you increase my faith in you and your Word. Let hearts around the world be opened to your Word, especially . . ." (Continue in your own words.)

Listen to Jesus.

Faith in my promises pleases me. I grant you what you seek, dear friend. Meditate upon my promises to you. What else is Jesus saying to you?

Ask God to show you how to live today.

"Throughout the day, Lord, bring to my mind one of your promises, that I may thank you for it and trust in you with all my heart. Thank you, precious Lord. Amen."

Wednesday, December 20, 2017

Know that God is present and ready to converse.

"Lord, let me not fear your presence in my life, especially now as I seek you in your Word."

Read the gospel: Luke 1:26–38.

In the sixth month the angel Gabriel was sent by God to a town in Galilee called Nazareth, to a virgin engaged to a man whose name was Joseph, of the house of David. The virgin's name was Mary. And he came to her and said, "Greetings, favored one! The Lord is with you." But she was much perplexed by his words and pondered what sort of greeting this might be. The angel said to her, "Do not be afraid, Mary, for you have found favor with God. And now, you will conceive in your womb and bear a son, and you will name him Jesus. He will be great, and will be called

the Son of the Most High, and the Lord God will give
to him the throne of his ancestor David. He will reign
over the house of Jacob forever, and of his kingdom
there will be no end." Mary said to the angel, "How
can this be, since I am a virgin?" The angel said to her,
"The Holy Spirit will come upon you, and the power
of the Most High will overshadow you; therefore the
child to be born will be holy; he will be called Son of
God. And now, your relative Elizabeth in her old age
has also conceived a son; and this is the sixth month
for her who was said to be barren. For nothing will be
impossible with God." Then Mary said, "Here am I, the
servant of the Lord; let it be with me according to your
word." Then the angel departed from her.

Notice what you think and feel as you read the gospel.

The angel Gabriel tells Mary not to be afraid, and then
announces how Mary will serve God in a way no other
has or ever will. She will conceive by the Holy Spirit
and bear a human son who would also be the Son
of God. Mary must have been overwhelmed by the
mystery and by the love of God. She must have been
overwhelmed the rest of her life as she pondered these
things in her heart.

Pray as you are led for yourself and others.

"Mary, thank you. Intercede for me with Jesus that I
may be as humble and willing to serve as you were.
Pray, too, for all those God has given me, especially . . ."
(Continue in your own words.)

Listen to Jesus.

You love my mother, and she is easy to love. I love you, too, beloved disciple. I hear your prayer today. Trust in me. What else is Jesus saying to you?

Ask God to show you how to live today.

"Keep me in your presence today, Lord, for I am prone to stray. Make your will clear to me. Praise to you, Lord Jesus Christ. Amen."

Thursday, December 21, 2017

Know that God is present and ready to converse.

"Bless me with faith, Lord, as I encounter you in your Word."

Read the gospel: Luke 1:39–45.

In those days Mary set out and went with haste to a Judean town in the hill country, where she entered the house of Zechariah and greeted Elizabeth. When Elizabeth heard Mary's greeting, the child leapt in her womb. And Elizabeth was filled with the Holy Spirit and exclaimed with a loud cry, "Blessed are you among women, and blessed is the fruit of your womb. And why has this happened to me, that the mother of my Lord comes to me? For as soon as I heard the sound of your greeting, the child in my womb leapt for joy. And blessed is she who believed that there would be a fulfillment of what was spoken to her by the Lord."

Notice what you think and feel as you read the gospel.

Elizabeth blesses Mary for believing God's message to her. Both are pregnant with sons who would change the world forever. God is with these women, working out his great plans through them. They don't know what's happening, but they rejoice in God.

Pray as you are led for yourself and others.

"Lord, I rejoice in your working in my life, even though I cannot know the future. All I need to know is that you are true and you are good. Let me please you by believing. I pray for these people I love . . ." (Continue in your own words.)

Listen to Jesus.

It is so simple to love me, child. If you love me, I will abide in you. When you are in the dark or hurting in any way, know that I am with you. I am all you need. What else is Jesus saying to you?

Ask God to show you how to live today.

"Let me leap for joy in your presence, Lord. Thank you. Amen."

Friday, December 22, 2017

Know that God is present and ready to converse.

"Let the Word of the Lord speak to my heart and change me into the person God wants me to be."

Read the gospel: Luke 1:46–56.

And Mary said,

> "My soul magnifies the Lord,
>> and my spirit rejoices in God my Savior,
> for he has looked with favor on the lowliness of
>> his servant.
>> Surely, from now on all generations will call
>> me blessed;
> for the Mighty One has done great things for me,
>> and holy is his name.
> His mercy is for those who fear him
>> from generation to generation.
> He has shown strength with his arm;
>> he has scattered the proud in the thoughts of
>> their hearts.
> He has brought down the powerful from their
>> thrones,
>> and lifted up the lowly;
> he has filled the hungry with good things,
>> and sent the rich away empty.
> He has helped his servant Israel,
>> in remembrance of his mercy,
> according to the promise he made to our ancestors,
>> to Abraham and to his descendants forever."

And Mary remained with her for about three months and then returned to her home.

Notice what you think and feel as you read the gospel.

Mary is very confident that God favors those who are weak, poor, and humble but scatters those who are strong, rich, and proud. She rejoices in God's mercy and faithfulness.

Pray as you are led for yourself and others.

"Oh, for the gift of prayer such as Mary had, Lord. Inspire me as you inspired her, that I may please you, know you, and love you as never before. Let others be drawn to holy prayer as well, namely . . ." (Continue in your own words.)

Listen to Jesus.

I like the time we spend together, dear one. The only agenda I have for you is loving me. When you love me, you become what I want you to be: a child of God. What else is Jesus saying to you?

Ask God to show you how to live today.

"Let me love and praise you in every moment of the day, Lord, and humbly serve you in the poor and the weak, whom you love. Amen."

Saturday, December 23, 2017

Know that God is present and ready to converse.

"Grant me silence to hear your Word, and then free my tongue to praise you, Lord."

Read the gospel: Luke 1:57–66.

Now the time came for Elizabeth to give birth, and she bore a son. Her neighbors and relatives heard that the Lord had shown his great mercy to her, and they rejoiced with her.

On the eighth day they came to circumcise the child, and they were going to name him Zechariah after his father. But his mother said, "No; he is to be called John." They said to her, "None of your relatives has this name." Then they began motioning to his father to find out what name he wanted to give him. He asked for a writing-tablet and wrote, "His name is John." And all of them were amazed. Immediately his mouth was opened and his tongue freed, and he began to speak, praising God. Fear came over all their neighbors, and all these things were talked about throughout the entire hill country of Judea. All who heard them pondered them and said, "What then will this child become?" For, indeed, the hand of the Lord was with him.

Notice what you think and feel as you read the gospel.

Zechariah and Elizabeth name their new baby boy John, despite the neighbors' and relatives' protests. When Zechariah regains his speech, they know God is working a plan. They had no idea.

Pray as you are led for yourself and others.

"Lord, I have no idea what you are doing in my life and in the lives of those you have given me. Let me praise you in faith and hope for future blessings for all of us, including . . ." (Continue in your own words.)

Listen to Jesus.

You tend to lose the big picture in the day-to-day events of your life. Dearly beloved, grasp that the kingdom of heaven is within you and that with God all things are possible. Now and forever. What else is Jesus telling you?

Ask God to show you how to live today.

"All right, Jesus. Today is enough for me. Stay with me and help me do what you would have me do. Amen."

FOURTH WEEK OF ADVENT

By his coming, Christ brought with him all newness.

St. Irenaeus
Against Heresies

Sunday, December 24, 2017
Fourth Sunday of Advent

Know that God is present and ready to converse.

"How can it be that you are here with me today, Lord? I am not worthy. I offer myself to you that I may learn to know you and love you through your Word."

Read the gospel: Luke 1:26–38.

In the sixth month the angel Gabriel was sent by God to a town in Galilee called Nazareth, to a virgin engaged to a man whose name was Joseph, of the house of David. The virgin's name was Mary. And he came to her and said, "Greetings, favored one! The Lord is with you." But she was much perplexed by his words and pondered what sort of greeting this might be. The angel said to her, "Do not be afraid, Mary, for you have found favor with God. And now, you will conceive in your womb and bear a son, and you will name him Jesus. He will be great, and will be called the Son of the Most High, and the Lord God will give to him the throne of his ancestor David. He will reign over the house of Jacob forever, and of his kingdom there will be no end." Mary said to the angel, "How can this be, since I am a virgin?" The angel said to her, "The Holy Spirit will come upon you, and the power of the Most High will overshadow you; therefore the child to be born will be holy; he will be called Son of God. And now, your relative Elizabeth in her old age has also conceived a son; and this is the sixth month for her who was said to be barren. For nothing will be impossible with God." Then Mary said, "Here am I, the servant of the Lord; let it be with me according to your word." Then the angel departed from her.

Notice what you think and feel as you read the gospel.

Mary was "much perplexed" by the message of the angel, and she hadn't yet even heard the amazing announcement that she would be overshadowed by the Most High and conceive a child who would be the Son of God. As she listened to the angel's amazing announcement, she must have felt the peace of God, for she answers so beautifully, so humbly, so trustingly as she gives herself to the Lord's will.

Pray as you are led for yourself and others.

"Lord, let your peace descend upon me this day, as I wait to celebrate again your birth. Let your peace fill the world tonight, that all may sense that the Messiah has come . . ." (Continue in your own words.)

Listen to Jesus.

I give you my peace, beloved. Let yourself become a child as you contemplate the mysterious, loving ways of my Father. What else is Jesus saying to you?

Ask God to show you how to live today.

"Let me shine with your peace, grace, and joy today, Lord. Be with me in all I do. Amen."

THE CHRISTMAS SEASON
THROUGH EPIPHANY

God, who is in love with us, draws us to himself with his tenderness, by being born poor and frail in our midst, as one of us. He is born in Bethlehem, which means "house of bread." In this way, he seems to tell us that he is born as bread for us; he enters our life to give us his life; he comes into our world to give us his love. He does not come to devour or to lord it over us, but instead to feed and serve us. There is a straight line between the manger and the cross where Jesus will become bread that is broken. It is the straight line of love that gives and saves, the love that brings light to our lives and peace to our hearts.

Pope Francis
December 24, 2016

Monday, December 25, 2017
The Nativity of the Lord

Know that God is present and ready to converse.

"Emmanuel, you have come. You are here. Praise to the Infant Jesus."

Read the gospel: John 1:1–18.

In the beginning was the Word, and the Word was with God, and the Word was God. He was in the beginning with God. All things came into being through him, and without him not one thing came into being. What has come into being in him was life, and the life was the light of all people. The light shines in the darkness, and the darkness did not overcome it.

There was a man sent from God, whose name was John. He came as a witness to testify to the light, so that all might believe through him. He himself was not the light, but he came to testify to the light. The true light, which enlightens everyone, was coming into the world.

He was in the world, and the world came into being through him; yet the world did not know him. He came to what was his own, and his own people did not accept him. But to all who received him, who believed in his name, he gave power to become children of God, who were born, not of blood or of the will of the flesh or of the will of man, but of God.

And the Word became flesh and lived among us, and we have seen his glory, the glory as of a father's only son, full of grace and truth. (John testified to him and cried out, "This was he of whom I said, 'He who comes after me ranks ahead of me because he was before me.'") From his fullness we have all received, grace upon grace. The law indeed was given through Moses; grace and truth came through Jesus Christ. No one has ever seen God. It is God the only Son, who is close to the Father's heart, who has made him known.

Notice what you think and feel as you read the gospel.

This passage reveals the cosmic, theological Jesus Christ in his mysterious relationship with God and humanity. He is the eternal Word, God's own self, Life, and Light, sent into a world of sin and darkness to gather a people for God the Father. Christ has made the Father known to us.

Pray as you are led for yourself and others.

"You have given me grace upon grace. Thank you. I pray that many hearts of those you have given me may be open to your graces . . ." (Continue in your own words.)

Listen to Jesus.

You are right to love and to care for others. That pleases me, beloved. If you love them, consider how much God loves them. Entrust them to God. What else is Jesus saying to you?

Ask God to show you how to live today.

"Let my heart and mind remain in awareness of your birth, glorious in its humility. Praise to you, Savior. Amen."

Tuesday, December 26, 2017
Saint Stephen, First Martyr

Know that God is present and ready to converse.

"Lord God of Hosts, you dwell on high, yet you are here with me now in my struggles and sufferings. Let me hear your holy Word, Father."

Read the gospel: Matthew 10:17–22.

Jesus said, "Beware of them, for they will hand you over to councils and flog you in their synagogues; and you will be dragged before governors and kings because of me, as a testimony to them and the Gentiles. When they hand you over, do not worry about how you are to speak or what you are to say; for what you are to say will be given to you at that time; for it is not you who speak, but the Spirit of your Father speaking through you. Brother will betray brother to death, and a father his child, and children will rise against parents and have them put to death; and you will be hated by all because of my name. But the one who endures to the end will be saved."

Notice what you think and feel as you read the gospel.

Persecution, betrayal, and hatred are part of witnessing to the Messiah, the Lord, Jesus Christ. Under duress, we are to not worry but trust the Holy Spirit to speak through us. The goal is to endure in faithfulness to the end, even unto death.

Pray as you are led for yourself and others.

"Lord, we have experienced rejection by the world for speaking of you. I pray we may be strengthened and informed by your Spirit, to endure to the end. I think of . . ." (Continue in your own words.)

Listen to Jesus.

When I chose you for my own, child, I ordained you to suffering that the world may know that you are mine. This is your glory, as it was mine. Know that in your dying body, my life grows, and beyond the end is eternal life. What else is Jesus saying to you?

Ask God to show you how to live today.

"Help me to view all persecution and rejection from your perspective, Lord. Let my suffering testify to you and give you glory. Your kingdom come! Amen."

Wednesday, December 27, 2017
Saint John, Apostle and Evangelist

Know that God is present
and ready to converse.

"You ask me to seek you, Lord, and so I do, and I find you here already. Glory to God."

Read the gospel: John 20:1a, 2–8.

Early on the first day of the week . . . Mary Magdalene came to the tomb and saw that the stone had been removed from the tomb. So she ran and went to Simon Peter and the other disciple, the one whom Jesus loved, and said to them, "They have taken the Lord out of the

tomb, and we do not know where they have laid him."
Then Peter and the other disciple set out and went
towards the tomb. The two were running together, but
the other disciple outran Peter and reached the tomb
first. He bent down to look in and saw the linen wrappings lying there, but he did not go in. Then Simon
Peter came, following him, and went into the tomb.
He saw the linen wrappings lying there, and the cloth
that had been on Jesus' head, not lying with the linen
wrappings but rolled up in a place by itself. Then the
other disciple, who reached the tomb first, also went
in, and he saw and believed.

Notice what you think and feel as you read the gospel.

John, who wrote this passage, describes himself as
the other disciple, which seems like modesty, yet he
also refers to himself as the "one whom Jesus loved,"
which almost seems like vanity. He's also the faster
runner, yet he defers to Peter, who enters the tomb
immediately. John is human, but he is right to center
his identity on Jesus' love for him.

Pray as you are led for yourself and others.

"Lord, let me be myself, the person you love, at all
times. Let those you have given me recognize their
own standing as beloved children of God . . ." (Continue in your own words.)

Listen to Jesus.

*You are my beloved disciple; I promise you that. I love all
uniquely and infinitely. I proved it on the Cross.* What else
is Jesus saying to you?

Ask God to show you how to live today.

"Lord, make me aware every moment that I am the disciple Jesus loves. Amen."

Thursday, December 28, 2017
Holy Innocents

Know that God is present
and ready to converse.

"God, you give us your Word, Jesus, your Son. Let it be sharper than a two-edged sword in me today, transforming me as you will."

Read the gospel: Matthew 2:13–18.

Now after they had left, an angel of the Lord appeared to Joseph in a dream and said, "Get up, take the child and his mother, and flee to Egypt, and remain there until I tell you; for Herod is about to search for the child, to destroy him." Then Joseph got up, took the child and his mother by night, and went to Egypt, and remained there until the death of Herod. This was to fulfill what had been spoken by the Lord through the prophet, "Out of Egypt I have called my son."

When Herod saw that he had been tricked by the wise men, he was infuriated, and he sent and killed all the children in and around Bethlehem who were two years old or under, according to the time that he had learned from the wise men. Then was fulfilled what had been spoken through the prophet Jeremiah:

"A voice was heard in Ramah,
    wailing and loud lamentation,
Rachel weeping for her children;

she refused to be consoled, because they are
no more."

Notice what you think and feel as you read the gospel.

I feel violence in the clash between good people and
evil people and horror at the death of the innocent
infants. God allows evil, with all its tragedy, as he
moves forward his unstoppable plan of salvation. He
will keep his promise, however mysterious his ways.

Pray as you are led for yourself and others.

"Lord, let me embrace your will, though it takes me
through the valley of the shadow of death, for you
are with me. Be also with those I remember now . . ."
(Continue in your words.)

Listen to Jesus.

*Give yourself entirely to me, and you have life no one can
take from you—no person, no devil, no circumstance. I am
the Way, the Truth, and the Life. Enter into the joy of the
Lord, my child.* What else is Jesus saying to you?

Ask God to show you how to live today.

"Help me to keep your hope foremost, relying upon
your promises, not succumbing to my fears. Thank
you, Mighty God. Amen."

Friday, December 29, 2017

Know that God is present and ready to converse.

"Lord, by your Word, by Jesus, you shed your light on me. I open myself to your light."

Read the gospel: Luke 2:22–35.

When the time came for their purification according to the law of Moses, they brought him up to Jerusalem to present him to the Lord (as it is written in the law of the Lord, "Every firstborn male shall be designated as holy to the Lord"), and they offered a sacrifice according to what is stated in the law of the Lord, "a pair of turtledoves or two young pigeons."

Now there was a man in Jerusalem whose name was Simeon; this man was righteous and devout, looking forward to the consolation of Israel, and the Holy Spirit rested on him. It had been revealed to him by the Holy Spirit that he would not see death before he had seen the Lord's Messiah. Guided by the Spirit, Simeon came into the temple; and when the parents brought in the child Jesus, to do for him what was customary under the law, Simeon took him in his arms and praised God, saying,

> "Master, now you are dismissing your servant in peace,
> according to your word;
> for my eyes have seen your salvation,
> which you have prepared in the presence of all peoples,
> a light for revelation to the Gentiles
> and for glory to your people Israel."

And the child's father and mother were amazed at what was being said about him. Then Simeon blessed them and said to his mother Mary, "This child is destined for the falling and the rising of many in Israel, and to be a sign that will be opposed so that the inner thoughts of many will be revealed—and a sword will pierce your own soul too."

Notice what you think and feel as you read the gospel.

Simeon is close to God, and he perceives through the Spirit and prophesies about the child Jesus and his mother: he will disrupt the world, and she too will be pierced.

Pray as you are led for yourself and others.

"Let me walk with you faithfully in the Spirit without fear, as Simeon and Mary did. Let your peace fall upon all those you have given me . . ." (Continue in your own words.)

Listen to Jesus.

In the world you too will have trouble, but don't be afraid because I have overcome the world. Walk with me, beloved. What else is Jesus saying to you?

Ask God to show you how to live today.

"Help me to walk step-by-step with you all day, doing what pleases you most. Thank you for your faithfulness to me, Jesus. Amen."

Saturday, December 30, 2017

Know that God is present and ready to converse.

"Lord, you make yourself known to your servants. Please number me among them."

Read the gospel: Luke 2:36–40.

There was also a prophet, Anna the daughter of Phanuel, of the tribe of Asher. She was of a great age, having lived with her husband for seven years after her marriage, then as a widow to the age of eighty-four. She never left the temple but worshipped there with fasting and prayer night and day. At that moment she came, and began to praise God and to speak about the child to all who were looking for the redemption of Jerusalem.

When they had finished everything required by the law of the Lord, they returned to Galilee, to their own town of Nazareth. The child grew and became strong, filled with wisdom; and the favor of God was upon him.

Notice what you think and feel as you read the gospel.

Like Simeon, Anna is a prophet because of her closeness with God. She learned to love being with God, night and day, and God rewarded her with a glimpse of the Redeemer.

Pray as you are led for yourself and others.

"God, give me Anna's love for you and teach me to fast and pray in a way that pleases you. I want to pray well

because I want you to bless the ones I pray for now . . ."
(Continue in your own words.)

Listen to Jesus.

I look upon the heart, child. Do you seek me with all your heart? Do you pray for others with a heart full of love? Do you persist in prayer? Ask me for what you need, and you shall have it. What else is Jesus saying to you?

Ask God to show you how to live today.

"Lord, help me to see where I fall short, so that I may seek from you the power to pray effectively. Amen."

Sunday, December 31, 2017
Holy Family of Jesus, Mary, and Joseph

Know that God is present
and ready to converse.

"Lord, I thank you for including me in your family. I sit at your feet to know you better."

Read the gospel: Luke 2:22–40.

When the time came for their purification according to the law of Moses, they brought Jesus up to Jerusalem to present him to the Lord (as it is written in the law of the Lord, "Every firstborn male shall be designated as holy to the Lord"), and they offered a sacrifice according to what is stated in the law of the Lord, "a pair of turtledoves or two young pigeons."

Now there was a man in Jerusalem whose name was Simeon; this man was righteous and devout, looking forward to the consolation of Israel, and the Holy Spirit rested on him. It had been revealed to him by the

Holy Spirit that he would not see death before he had seen the Lord's Messiah. Guided by the Spirit, Simeon came into the temple; and when the parents brought in the child Jesus, to do for him what was customary under the law, Simeon took him in his arms and praised God, saying,

> "Master, now you are dismissing your servant in peace,
> according to your word;
> for my eyes have seen your salvation,
> which you have prepared in the presence of all peoples,
> a light for revelation to the Gentiles
> and for glory to your people Israel."

And the child's father and mother were amazed at what was being said about him. Then Simeon blessed them and said to his mother Mary, "This child is destined for the falling and the rising of many in Israel, and to be a sign that will be opposed so that the inner thoughts of many will be revealed—and a sword will pierce your own soul too."

There was also a prophet, Anna the daughter of Phanuel, of the tribe of Asher. She was of a great age, having lived with her husband for seven years after her marriage, then as a widow to the age of eighty-four. She never left the temple but worshipped there with fasting and prayer night and day. At that moment she came, and began to praise God and to speak about the child to all who were looking for the redemption of Jerusalem.

When they had finished everything required by the law of the Lord, they returned to Galilee, to their own town of Nazareth. The child grew and became strong, filled with wisdom; and the favor of God was upon him.

Notice what you think and feel as you read the gospel.

Seeking merely to present the infant Jesus according to the law, Mary and Joseph witness marvelous things in the Temple and hear surprising prophesies from two ancient servants of God. Afterward, the Holy Family returns to Nazareth. In the midst of God's mysterious workings, they simply raised their boy day by day. God was with their son.

Pray as you are led for yourself and others.

"Be with me and mine, Lord, as we seek to meet our responsibilities every day. Bless our efforts, especially . . ." (Continue in your own words.)

Listen to Jesus.

Seek me first, beloved, and we will live every day in love. Every day will be new for us. You will grow in strength, wisdom, and the favor of God. What else is Jesus saying to you?

Ask God to show you how to live today.

"What you want is what I want, Lord. And when I resist, bend my will to your own. Amen."

Monday, January 1, 2018
Solemnity of the Blessed Virgin Mary, Mother of God

Know that God is present and ready to converse.

"Lord God Almighty, you humble yourself to be with us and to speak with us because you love us. Let me receive your Word now and return your love."

Read the gospel: Luke 2:16–21.

So the shepherds went with haste and found Mary and Joseph, and the child lying in the manger. When they saw this, they made known what had been told them about this child; and all who heard it were amazed at what the shepherds told them. But Mary treasured all these words and pondered them in her heart. The shepherds returned, glorifying and praising God for all they had heard and seen, as it had been told them. After eight days had passed, it was time to circumcise the child; and he was called Jesus, the name given by the angel before he was conceived in the womb.

Notice what you think and feel as you read the gospel.

God sent his angels to tell the shepherds about the birth of Jesus. He chose the shepherds to be witnesses to the amazing event—God chooses the humble, the poor, the simple to do his will.

Pray as you are led for yourself and others.

"Let me encounter Jesus as humbly as the poor shepherds, Lord, and send me out to spread your love and serve those you have given me . . ." (Continue in your own words.)

Listen to Jesus.

You may learn the ways of God, dear disciple, by meditating on the words of God. I will show you everything you need to know, but you must look to me faithfully. Turn to me in your great need. What else is Jesus saying to you?

Ask God to show you how to live today.

"Teach me, Lord; let me be your student attentive to all you say in all the people and events of my life, starting today. Amen."

Tuesday, January 2, 2018

Know that God is present and ready to converse.

"Let me learn from you, Holy Spirit, that I may have an answer to any who are trying to trap me. Glory to you, O Lord."

Read the gospel: John 1:19–28.

This is the testimony given by John when the Jews sent priests and Levites from Jerusalem to ask him, "Who are you?" He confessed and did not deny it, but confessed, "I am not the Messiah." And they asked him, "What then? Are you Elijah?" He said, "I am not." "Are you the prophet?" He answered, "No." Then they said to him, "Who are you? Let us have an answer for those who sent us. What do you say about yourself?" He said,

"I am the voice of one crying out in the wilderness,
'Make straight the way of the Lord,'"

as the prophet Isaiah said.

Now they had been sent from the Pharisees. They asked him, "Why then are you baptizing if you are neither the Messiah, nor Elijah, nor the prophet?" John answered them, "I baptize with water. Among you stands one whom you do not know, the one who is coming after me; I am not worthy to untie the thong of his sandal." This took place in Bethany across the Jordan where John was baptizing.

Notice what you think and feel as you read the gospel.

Except for the middle paragraph quoting scripture, each paragraph in this passage contains four negatives as the priests try to trap John in his words. He simply says, no, I am not the Messiah, and quotes Isaiah, "I am the voice of one crying in the wilderness." In the final paragraph, John speaks the most powerful negative of all: "I am *not* worthy to untie the thong of his sandal."

Pray as you are led for yourself and others.

"Lord, I am not worthy either, yet you have called me to follow you and love others. As I follow, Lord, I pray with all my heart for the needs of others, including . . ." (Continue in your own words.)

Listen to Jesus.

Sometimes the simple truth is "no." Try to speak the simple truth in all your affairs, child. Know that all God's promises are "yes" in me. What else is Jesus saying to you?

Ask God to show you how to live today.

"I want to be a more honest, simple, straightforward person, Lord, to please you. Give me opportunities and teach me to do it. Amen."

Wednesday, January 3, 2018

Know that God is present and ready to converse.

"You are always with me, Lord. Thank you. Let me turn to you now with my heart, mind, soul, and spirit so that I may hear and be converted."

Read the gospel: John 1:29–34.

The next day John the Baptist saw Jesus coming towards him and declared, "Here is the Lamb of God who takes away the sin of the world! This is he of whom I said, 'After me comes a man who ranks ahead of me because he was before me.' I myself did not know him; but I came baptizing with water for this reason, that he might be revealed to Israel." And John testified, "I saw the Spirit descending from heaven like a dove, and it remained on him. I myself did not know him, but the one who sent me to baptize with water said to me, 'He on whom you see the Spirit descend and remain is the one who baptizes with the Holy Spirit.' And I myself have seen and have testified that this is the Son of God."

Notice what you think and feel as you read the gospel.

John recognizes Jesus even as he approaches, calling him the Lamb of God. John says he saw the Spirit descending upon Jesus, a sign to him that Jesus is the Son of God.

Pray as you are led for yourself and others.

"John's ministry of water baptism gave way to Jesus' ministry of baptism with the Holy Spirit. Baptize me and all those you have given me in your Spirit, Lord! . . ." (Continue in your own words.)

Listen to Jesus.

Those who walk by the Spirit do not always know where they are going, but you may know that I always go with you. You ask me for the Holy Spirit. I grant your prayer. Receive the Holy Spirit. What else is Jesus saying to you?

Ask God to show you how to live today.

"Guide me with your Spirit today. Make me free to abandon habit, to do inspired acts of love for God and for others. Amen."

Thursday, January 4, 2018

Know that God is present and ready to converse.

"Jesus, I have found you as my Savior, but you have known me all along."

Read the gospel: John 1:35–42.

The next day John again was standing with two of his disciples, and as he watched Jesus walk by, he exclaimed, "Look, here is the Lamb of God!" The two disciples heard him say this, and they followed Jesus. When Jesus turned and saw them following, he said to them, "What are you looking for?" They said to him,

"Rabbi" (which translated means Teacher), "where are you staying?" He said to them, "Come and see." They came and saw where he was staying, and they remained with him that day. It was about four o'clock in the afternoon. One of the two who heard John speak and followed him was Andrew, Simon Peter's brother. He first found his brother Simon and said to him, "We have found the Messiah" (which is translated Anointed). He brought Simon to Jesus, who looked at him and said, "You are Simon son of John. You are to be called Cephas" (which is translated Peter).

Notice what you think and feel as you read the gospel.

John calls Jesus the Lamb of God, and immediately John's disciples follow Jesus, who invites them over for a visit. When Andrew tells his brother Simon that they have found the Messiah, he brings him to Jesus, who already knows him. Jesus tells Simon he will be called Cephas, Peter, the rock.

Pray as you are led for yourself and others.

"Lord, you know everything about me. Give me what I need. Just draw me, and all those you have given me, to yourself . . ." (Continue in your own words.)

Listen to Jesus.

Everyone in the kingdom of God has a new name already inscribed, ready to be revealed, for you have been known and loved by God for eternity, my child. What else is Jesus saying to you?

Ask God to show you how to live today.

"Help me to follow you closely. Help me get to know you as you know me, Lord. Thank you. Amen."

Friday, January 5, 2018

Know that God is present and ready to converse.

"Jesus, King of Kings, Lord of Lords, you allow me to be with you now. Someday I will see the angels ascending and descending upon the Son of Man."

Read the gospel: John 1:43–51.

The next day Jesus decided to go to Galilee. He found Philip and said to him, "Follow me." Now Philip was from Bethsaida, the city of Andrew and Peter. Philip found Nathanael and said to him, "We have found him about whom Moses in the law and also the prophets wrote, Jesus son of Joseph from Nazareth." Nathanael said to him, "Can anything good come out of Nazareth?" Philip said to him, "Come and see." When Jesus saw Nathanael coming towards him, he said of him, "Here is truly an Israelite in whom there is no deceit!" Nathanael asked him, "Where did you come to know me?" Jesus answered, "I saw you under the fig tree before Philip called you." Nathanael replied, "Rabbi, you are the Son of God! You are the King of Israel!" Jesus answered, "Do you believe because I told you that I saw you under the fig tree? You will see greater things than these." And he said to him, "Very truly, I tell you, you will see heaven opened and the angels of God ascending and descending upon the Son of Man."

Notice what you think and feel as you read the gospel.

Nathanael is skeptical when Philip tells him that they have found the one foretold in Moses and the prophets. "Out of Nazareth?" Nathanael asks. Yet he, like Philip, Andrew, and Peter, is from Bethsaida, hardly a major city. Jesus pays Nathanael a wonderful compliment, again showing that he knows the heart of everyone. Nathanael believes.

Pray as you are led for yourself and others.

"Take all guile from my heart, Lord, so that I can please you and follow you closely. In your love, let me serve others by prayer and service. I think of . . ." (Continue in your own words.)

Listen to Jesus.

I will give you the opportunity to show love today, dear disciple. The love you show will be our love, not yours alone and not mine alone. This is how I work in the hearts of people. What else is Jesus saying to you?

Ask God to show you how to live today.

"Give me the love that is both yours and mine, Lord, and help me to apply it generously today. Amen."

Saturday, January 6, 2018

Know that God is present and ready to converse.

"Holy Spirit, Creator God, author of the Word of God, Spouse of Mary, the Mother of God, open my eyes and my heart to God right now."

Read the gospel: Mark 1:7–11.

John proclaimed, "The one who is more powerful than I is coming after me; I am not worthy to stoop down and untie the thong of his sandals. I have baptized you with water; but he will baptize you with the Holy Spirit."

In those days Jesus came from Nazareth of Galilee and was baptized by John in the Jordan. And just as he was coming up out of the water, he saw the heavens torn apart and the Spirit descending like a dove on him. And a voice came from heaven, "You are my Son, the Beloved; with you I am well pleased."

Notice what you think and feel as you read the gospel.

Through Jesus, God is performing the most loving act possible—he is saving the human race from sin and death. Jesus brings mercy, forgiveness, atonement, and eternal life for whomever will receive him. The Father, Son, and Holy Spirit are united in this endeavor. Praise God.

Pray as you are led for yourself and others.

"Father, Son, and Holy Spirit, I long to join your circle of love. Let that be the goal of my day and my lifetime, never faltering. With you, that is possible. I pray the same for all those you have given me and think particularly of . . ." (Continue in your own words.)

Listen to Jesus.

I rejoice that you desire my love, my friend. What you desire you shall have, for you are asking for what is of supreme

*good. Through love and love alone you enter into fellowship
with God.* What else is Jesus saying to you?

Ask God to show you how to live today.

"Let my love and desire for you grow today, so that
I will see you in anyone who needs some help, and I
will act in love. Amen."

Sunday, January 7, 2018
Epiphany of the Lord

Know that God is present
and ready to converse.

"Lord above, you have come down to earth, and you
stop here with me as I read and pray. I praise you."

Read the gospel: Matthew 2:1–12.

In the time of King Herod, after Jesus was born in Bethlehem of Judea, wise men from the East came to Jerusalem, asking, "Where is the child who has been born
king of the Jews? For we observed his star at its rising, and have come to pay him homage." When King
Herod heard this, he was frightened, and all Jerusalem
with him; and calling together all the chief priests and
scribes of the people, he inquired of them where the
Messiah was to be born. They told him, "In Bethlehem
of Judea; for so it has been written by the prophet:

> 'And you, Bethlehem, in the land of Judah,
>   are by no means least among the rulers
>   of Judah;
> for from you shall come a ruler
>   who is to shepherd my people Israel.'"

Then Herod secretly called for the wise men and learned from them the exact time when the star had appeared. Then he sent them to Bethlehem, saying, "Go and search diligently for the child; and when you have found him, bring me word so that I may also go and pay him homage." When they had heard the king, they set out; and there, ahead of them, went the star that they had seen at its rising, until it stopped over the place where the child was. When they saw that the star had stopped, they were overwhelmed with joy. On entering the house, they saw the child with Mary his mother; and they knelt down and paid him homage. Then, opening their treasure chests, they offered him gifts of gold, frankincense, and myrrh. And having been warned in a dream not to return to Herod, they left for their own country by another road.

Notice what you think and feel as you read the gospel.

When the star stops, the wise men are filled with joy. How mysterious their foreknowledge of this event, their collaboration, their journey! They seem to have understood what was happening. They even respond to the warning in a dream and do not return to Herod.

Pray as you are led for yourself and others.

"Lord, lead me to you and let me worship you with joy. I pray that all those you have given me learn the joy of worshipping God, incarnate in Jesus, the child born in Bethlehem . . ." (Continue in your own words.)

Listen to Jesus.

If you love me, child, you will seek me. If you seek me, you will find me. When you do, you will be filled with joy that

*transcends all your struggles and suffering. Find me in your
heart, my love.* What else is Jesus saying to you?

Ask God to show you how to live today.

"Lord, I am overwhelmed by the mystery of worship,
this prayer relationship we have. Please keep me going
steadily toward you. What gift may I give you today?
Amen.

A Special Gift for You

AN EXCERPT FROM *THREE MOMENTS OF THE DAY: PRAYING WITH THE HEART OF JESUS* BY CHRISTOPHER S. COLLINS, S.J.

Stumbling into the Three Moments

> The favors of the Lord are not exhausted,
> his mercies are not spent;
> They are renewed each morning,
> so great is his faithfulness.
>
> —Lamentations 3:22–23

I had never paid attention to images of the Heart of Jesus before I joined the Society of Jesus (Jesuits). Even though I grew up in a solid Catholic family and went to Catholic schools all my life, the Sacred Heart never penetrated my dense little consciousness.

But soon after I joined the Jesuits at the age of twenty-three, I read a book by Fr. Pedro Arrupe, an earlier superior general who played a major role in reforming and updating the Jesuit Order after the Second Vatican Council.

Fr. Arrupe helped our order to get in sync with the times. But Fr. Arrupe was also critical of the times, believing that Catholics as a whole and Jesuits in particular had lost touch with what might be called a *devotional imagination*. He reminded us that devotion to the Heart of Christ—that is, devotion to the love God shows us in the flesh of his Son whose loving Heart was pierced on the Cross—should remain the center of our lives. It is Christ's Heart that speaks of God's will for us. God's love, demonstrated in the flesh by Jesus, is the source of our hope. Arrupe even went so far as to say that the renewal of the devotion to the Sacred Heart would be a sign of the renewal of the Society of Jesus. As a brand-new Jesuit, I took note of this, though honestly I didn't really know what it meant and what it would soon come to mean in my own life.

Only a few months later, in bleak midwinter, I was sent by my novice master to Pine Ridge, South Dakota. This was not a vacation. I had accepted a mission to teach students at Red Cloud Indian School, which is a work of our mission on the reservation there. I was also commissioned to drive the school bus in the afternoons and do odd jobs around the place.

Now, any teacher will tell you that coming to a school in the middle of the year is difficult under the best of circumstances. However, I had taught high school for two years, and so I thought I would probably be successful in the classroom here. I was mistaken.

Because of the cultural and religious differences between the Native American students and their mostly white teachers, many students did not trust their teachers. This was especially true of me, the newcomer. Every day after I had finished teaching and driving the afternoon bus, I would come back to the community chapel and just sit there. I thought I was praying, but in reality I was just talking to myself about my woes.

I was being beaten in the classroom day in and day out. What I eagerly wanted to give them, these Lakota teenagers did not want. They had grown up on the reservation with a suspicion of white people in general and of priests and religious in particular. Many associated Christianity with the forces of colonialism that had oppressed them and left them bereft of their culture and their way of life. This made sense. But it also put up barriers. The students and I were both carrying a lot of historical baggage.

At first I was angry with the kids: *What's their problem? How can they be so disrespectful and ungrateful?* Then I would be angry with their parents for not raising them right. Soon, however, I turned that angry judging of others onto myself. I had much to accuse myself of. The problem wasn't so much with the students but with the teacher. *If you knew what you were doing in there,* I said to myself, *you would be able to handle the classroom. You thought you were a successful teacher already, but it's clear now that you're a fraud. If you weren't so lazy and ill prepared, you might be able to come up with a lesson plan that would work!*

Encountering the Sacred Heart

Obviously, my afternoons in the chapel judging the kids and their parents and then berating myself made for some pretty messy prayer times. But then one day as I sat in the chapel, I noticed a statue outside the door to the hallway, just beyond the tabernacle. For some reason this little painted plaster image drew my attention.

It was my first personal encounter with the Sacred Heart. Jesus was standing there with his Heart opened up, vulnerable, on the outside of his body. The Heart was pierced and bloody, and the plaster itself was dinged up quite a bit. I noticed his hands, too; one pointed to his heart, the other beckoned to me. There he stood, looking at me with such intense love; it was as if he was speaking directly to me, saying, "This is the way I live. This is the way I love. Truly, this is the only way to love. You can do it. You must do it. There is no other way."

As I looked at the statue, what drew me in was the pierced Heart. That's how my heart felt. Mine was getting pierced in smaller ways than Jesus' Heart but in very real ways nonetheless. I had given myself to this religious vocation. And now I wanted to share what had been happening in my heart with kids who I knew desperately needed to hear some good news, and yet they wanted none of it. Not only was I proving to be a lame teacher but also that perhaps my whole vocation was for nothing. As they rejected me every day, my students were in a small but real way piercing my heart. I could see Jesus' Heart had been pierced long before mine, but maybe his Heart was continuing to be pierced right along with mine. I suddenly saw that I was not alone.

More important, I began to situate this whole context into a larger framework. The piercings my students had undergone in their own lives were far greater than anything I was feeling. I started to see all of this—my own suffering, the suffering of those around me, and the suffering found in the whole of human history—as marked by wounds of various degrees and kinds. And now I was beginning to see all of it in light of the pierced Heart of Christ.

But that Heart was more than just pierced. I also saw the fire emerging out of it. Even though the piercings are real, continuous wounds, they do not destroy his Heart. He could take the piercings, all the way to death, even, and still live. And it wasn't a matter of taking the pain in some heroic, stoic, tough-guy way. I could see in a new way that Jesus had a way of transforming these sufferings into fire, into life, and into love. The piercings and the fire of that Heart had started to sink into my imagination, and I began to see with the eyes of my own heart how the piercings and the fire go together. They are not contradictory. In fact, the power and brightness of the fire is made possible only by the piercings. . . .

Once I began to see the Sacred Heart in this way, it became clear to me that this was all I needed. I saw, and still see, that this is all there is. This is the whole of reality. The point of our lives is love. There is no love without piercings along the way, but the piercings will not do us in. I will be wounded along the way living this life, living this vocation, but I can remain on fire. There is a fire that will not be quenched if I keep my heart open, if I resist the temptations to shut down, to defend, and to hide. This is Jesus. His whole mission has always been to open up the Heart of God to the world and not flinch in doing so. . . .

Rediscover the Daily Prayer of the Heart

Over time, some Jesuit friends and I adopted a method of prayer that we later discovered had been established long before we took up the practice. This approach involves offering my heart and my life to God at three separate "moments" of each day.

At the beginning of the day, I say to Jesus, "I want to live this day, and all that's in it, not in isolation but with you. I want to offer what's in my heart to what's in your Heart."

At the end of the day, I take another moment to look back and see how it's gone. This prayer, or Examen, is based on one of the ways of praying taught by St. Ignatius of Loyola in his Spiritual Exercises. This is a simple act of using memory to pay attention to what actually happened in the day. Little by little, I developed a habit of speaking to Jesus about all that is ordinary in my life. As I continued this daily practice of engaging in brief exchanges every morning and evening, it began to change how I looked at the world.

The third "moment" covers the spiritual reality of the whole day. We might think of this moment as a continuation of the celebration of the Eucharist, the source and summit of our lives. Whether or not we attended Mass on a particular day, the ordinariness of everyday life is best understood in light of this "moment" of prayer in which the whole Church engages all over the world, every day. Although you and I cannot be physically present at every moment and in every place this prayer is being offered, we are a part of this mystery. What goes on in the Eucharist gives me a framework for understanding and making choices in daily life that will lead me out of isolation and into relationship, into dialogue, and into friendship with God.

This "three moments" approach to prayer is not about "punching the clock" with God; we are not God's employees. We are his children. And so, we offer our lives to God, day by day, in the same way that Jesus offered his life and days to the Father. This is a way of praying and seeing the world that starts to make our daily lives much more intimate, as places of genuine encounter with God. Our day-to-day living, seen from within this way of praying, becomes a matter of one heart being offered to another. What sparked this discovery for me was the "discovery" of what I came to realize was called the Sacred Heart of Jesus. . . .

As you start praying like this, little by little, you will get in the habit of speaking to Jesus about all that is ordinary in your life. Then you'll begin to realize that by speaking about it to him, things are starting to change—or you are changing. Everything is changing. Things might not have gotten fixed the way you asked or expected, but they did get fixed. These brief exchanges of speaking and listening during the day will change the landscape of your life. This prayer practice can change how you see the world.

The Apostleship of Prayer (The Pope's Worldwide Prayer Network) is an international pontifical prayer ministry served by the Jesuits that reaches more than 35 million members worldwide through its popular website, *ApostleshipofPrayer.org*, and through talks, conferences, publications, and retreats. The Apostleship's mission is to encourage Christians to make a daily offering of themselves to God in union with the Sacred Heart of Jesus.

Douglas Leonard, who compiles *Sacred Reading*, served as the executive director of the Apostleship of Prayer in the United States from 2006 to 2016. He earned a bachelor's degree in English in 1976, a master's degree in English in 1977, and a PhD in English in 1981, all from the University of Wisconsin-Madison. Leonard also has served in higher education, professional development, publishing, and instructional design as an executive, writer, editor, educator, and consultant.